AMERICA'S GLOBAL ODYSSEY

Pioneering New Horizons, Shaping Tomorrow.

Introduction:

Welcome to "America's Global Odyssey: Pioneering New Horizons, Shaping Tomorrow." This expedition embarks on a profound exploration of America's enduring influence on the world stage. As we navigate the intricate tapestry of geopolitics, economics, technology, and societal dynamics, we unveil the myriad facets that define America's pivotal role in shaping the future of our interconnected world.

From the zenith of historical dominance to the challenges posed by emerging global competitors, environmental transformations, and the ethical landscapes of space exploration, each chapter in this odyssey meticulously dissects the themes that underpin America's presence in the contemporary global narrative.

This compelling narrative transcends mere analysis; it's an invitation to traverse the depths of America's impact, uncovering the subtleties and prospects that shape its role in an ever-evolving world. Our journey navigates critical territories including cultural diplomacy, cybersecurity governance, sustainable investment, and the ethical dimensions of emergent technologies, fostering a comprehensive understanding of America's position within the interconnected global fabric.

"America's Global Odyssey" is more than a recounting of historical footprints; it's a narrative that intertwines America's legacy, challenges, and aspirations with the destinies of nations worldwide. Thought-provoking, engaging, and insightful, this expedition serves as a beacon, illuminating the intricacies of America's global presence and offering a vision for a collective, resilient, and inclusive tomorrow on a global scale. Join us on this odyssey as we unveil the complexities and aspirations that define America's pursuit of pioneering new horizons and shaping the landscape of tomorrow.

CHAPTER 1: INTRODUCTION - AMERICA'S HISTORICAL DOMINANCE

The story of America's ascent to global prominence is one intertwined with ambition, innovation, and resilience. From its early days as a fledgling nation to its meteoric rise as a superpower, the United States has wielded considerable influence across the world stage.

This chapter delves into the historical journey that propelled America to unparalleled heights of power and authority. It explores the key milestones, pivotal moments, and defining decisions that shaped America's dominance, spanning economic, political, and cultural spheres.

From the industrial revolution that catapulted the nation into an economic powerhouse to pivotal historical events like World War II, where America's intervention redefined global geopolitics, this chapter sets the stage by chronicling the factors that contributed to America's emergence as a leading force in the world.

However, as the world evolves and new global challenges emerge, the foundation of America's historical dominance faces scrutiny. The subsequent chapters will examine the shifting dynamics that challenge this historical narrative, exploring whether America's position as a global powerhouse remains unassailable or if significant changes are on the horizon.

CHAPTER 2: THE RISE OF GLOBAL COMPETITORS

The landscape of global power is experiencing a profound transformation, marked by the ascent of formidable competitors challenging America's traditional dominance. This chapter explores the emergence of rival powers and their impact on the geopolitical balance.

China stands at the forefront of this shift, rapidly ascending as a formidable economic force and a key player in international affairs. Its strategic investments, technological advancements, and assertive foreign policies have propelled it into a position of significant influence, posing a direct challenge to America's supremacy.

Simultaneously, other nations, including India, Brazil, and Russia, among others, have also strengthened their global presence, diversifying the centers of power in the international arena.

This chapter analyzes the economic, technological, and geopolitical strategies employed by these rising powers, examining their motivations, strengths, and potential vulnerabilities. It delves into the implications of this shifting landscape on America's global standing, exploring whether cooperation, competition, or conflict will define the interactions between established and emerging powers.

As the global stage witnesses the rise of these new contenders, this chapter seeks to unravel the complexities of a world where multiple centers of power vie for influence, potentially altering the dynamics of global politics and economics.

CHAPTER 3: ECONOMIC CHALLENGES AND TRADE DYNAMICS

The economic landscape is a critical determinant of a nation's global standing. This chapter delves into the intricate web of challenges and dynamics shaping America's economic position in the evolving global scenario.

At the heart of this discussion lies the intricate dance of trade dynamics. Over decades, America has played a central role in shaping global trade patterns, fostering alliances, and wielding economic influence. However, this landscape is undergoing significant shifts.

The rise of protectionist sentiments, trade disputes, and geopolitical tensions has ushered in a new era of economic uncertainty. The chapter examines how these factors have impacted America's economic relationships with key partners and competitors. It explores the ramifications of trade policies, tariffs, and bilateral agreements on the nation's economic prowess and global alliances.

Moreover, the digital economy and technological advancements have altered traditional trade paradigms. The emergence of e-commerce, digital currencies, and data-driven industries presents both opportunities and challenges for America's economic leadership.

Furthermore, economic disparities, income inequality, and challenges in workforce development pose internal hurdles to sustaining economic supremacy. This chapter scrutinizes these domestic challenges and their implications for America's ability to maintain a competitive edge on the global economic stage.

In understanding these economic intricacies, this chapter seeks to unravel the complex interplay between domestic policies, global trade dynamics, and technological innovations, assessing their collective impact on America's role as a global economic powerhouse.

CHAPTER 4: POLITICAL FRAGMENTATION AND ITS IMPACT

In the midst of evolving global dynamics, America grapples with internal political fragmentation that reverberates on the international stage. This chapter delves into the fractures within the nation's political landscape and their repercussions on its global influence.

Polarization and ideological divisions have intensified, shaping policy-making and challenging the coherence of America's diplomatic initiatives. This chapter scrutinizes how these internal rifts affect the nation's ability to present a united front in international affairs, impacting its credibility and effectiveness in global governance.

The chapter examines the implications of a divided political environment on foreign policy decisions, alliances, and international engagements. It explores how divergent ideologies influence America's stance on critical global issues, including climate change, security alliances, and human rights, among others.

Furthermore, the erosion of trust in institutions, coupled with challenges to democratic norms, poses significant questions about America's role as a bastion of democracy on the global stage. This section navigates through these challenges, assessing their implications for America's soft power and moral authority in shaping global agendas.

Ultimately, this chapter aims to dissect the ramifications of political fragmentation on America's ability to navigate complex global challenges cohesively, emphasizing the interplay between internal discord and its consequential impact on the nation's global standing and influence.

CHAPTER 5: TECHNOLOGICAL EVOLUTION AND THE RACE FOR INNOVATION

The accelerating pace of technological advancement has become a defining factor in the global power equation. This chapter explores America's historical prowess in innovation and its current position in the race for technological supremacy amidst a rapidly evolving landscape.

The United States has been a pioneering force in technological innovation, spearheading breakthroughs in sectors such as information technology, biotechnology, artificial intelligence, and space exploration. However, the competitive landscape is evolving as other nations invest heavily in research and development, narrowing the gap in technological capabilities.

This chapter assesses the factors influencing America's innovation ecosystem, including investments in research, intellectual property rights, regulatory frameworks, and collaboration between the private and public sectors. It delves into the strengths and vulnerabilities of America's innovation infrastructure, scrutinizing its capacity to retain leadership in crucial technological domains.

Moreover, the ethical dimensions of technological advancements, such as privacy concerns, data security, and the responsible use of emerging technologies, are pivotal in shaping public trust and global perceptions.

The emergence of new global hubs for innovation and the internationalization of research and development raise questions about America's continued dominance in this sphere.

Through this exploration, the chapter aims to dissect the evolving landscape of technological innovation, evaluating its impact on America's global competitiveness and the strategies required to maintain leadership in an era defined by rapid technological evolution.

CHAPTER 6: CULTURAL INFLUENCE AMIDST GLOBALIZATION

In the intricate tapestry of global influence, culture acts as a potent force shaping perceptions, ideologies, and soft power. This chapter delves into America's historical cultural impact and examines its current position in a world increasingly connected by globalization.

The United States has been a cultural powerhouse, exporting its music, movies, literature, and ideals across continents. American pop culture, with its Hollywood movies, popular music, and technological innovations, has traditionally held a pervasive influence, shaping global trends and lifestyles.

However, the landscape is evolving. This chapter navigates through the changing dynamics where diverse cultures, propelled by technological advancements and digital connectivity, are gaining prominence. It analyzes the impact of streaming platforms, social media, and the internet on the dissemination of cultural narratives, challenging America's historical dominance.

Moreover, questions arise about cultural diplomacy, soft power, and the projection of American values in an increasingly multipolar world. The chapter examines how cultural representation, diversity, and inclusivity shape perceptions of American identity and influence.

Simultaneously, the rise of regional and local cultural expressions around the globe raises inquiries about the homogenization versus diversification of global cultural landscapes.

By dissecting these cultural shifts, this chapter aims to evaluate America's evolving role in shaping global cultural dynamics and the strategies necessary to maintain cultural relevance and influence in an interconnected and diverse world.

CHAPTER 7: MILITARY STRENGTH IN A CHANGING WORLD

Amidst a rapidly evolving global landscape, the role of military strength remains a crucial determinant of a nation's power and influence. This chapter explores America's historical military dominance and assesses its position in a world witnessing geopolitical transformations.

The United States has long been a military superpower, boasting a formidable arsenal and global military presence. Its military prowess has shaped international security architectures and underpinned alliances, projecting both deterrence and intervention capabilities across the globe.

However, the nature of conflicts and security threats is evolving. This chapter delves into the changing dynamics of warfare, including cyber threats, asymmetrical warfare, and the emergence of non-state actors. It examines how these shifts challenge traditional military doctrines and strategies, prompting a reassessment of America's military posture.

Furthermore, the geopolitical landscape is witnessing the rise of new centers of military power. Nations like China, with significant military investments and modernization efforts, are altering the balance of military influence.

The chapter evaluates the implications of these changes on America's military strategy, defense investments, and global military engagements. It scrutinizes the challenges of maintaining military superiority in an era of technological advancements, fiscal constraints, and complex security threats.

Additionally, the role of alliances and multilateral cooperation in shaping collective security frameworks is a critical aspect analyzed within this chapter.

Through a comprehensive exploration, this chapter aims to dissect the evolving dynamics of military strength and its impact on America's global standing, strategizing the paths necessary to adapt to a changing security landscape.

CHAPTER 8: ENVIRONMENTAL CONCERNS AND GEOPOLITICAL SHIFTS

The interconnectedness between environmental issues and geopolitics has become increasingly evident, reshaping global power dynamics. This chapter delves into the intricate relationship between environmental challenges and their impact on global geopolitics, including America's role in addressing these concerns.

Climate change, resource scarcity, and environmental degradation pose complex challenges transcending national borders. The chapter scrutinizes how these challenges intersect with geopolitics, influencing alliances, conflicts, and global power structures.

America's historical stance on environmental policies, its participation in international agreements, and its influence on global environmental agendas are under scrutiny. The chapter assesses the implications of the nation's environmental policies on its global reputation and leadership in addressing climate change and sustainability.

Moreover, the competition for natural resources, including water, energy, and minerals, is increasingly becoming a focal point in geopolitical strategies. This chapter navigates through the implications of resource scarcity and environmental stressors on international relations, potential conflicts, and cooperation among nations.

Additionally, the rising awareness and advocacy for environmental justice and the role of civil society and grassroots movements in shaping environmental policies are crucial aspects analyzed in this chapter.

By dissecting these environmental challenges within a geopolitical framework, this chapter aims to evaluate the implications for America's global role and the strategies necessary to navigate the shifting geopolitical landscape amidst growing environmental concerns.

CHAPTER 9: IMMIGRATION, DIVERSITY, AND NATIONAL IDENTITY

The narrative of immigration, diversity, and national identity is integral to understanding America's societal fabric and its global image. This chapter delves into the complexities surrounding these themes and their impact on America's perception and position in the global arena.

Throughout its history, America has been a melting pot of diverse cultures and identities, shaped by waves of immigration. This chapter explores the historical significance of immigration in fostering innovation, economic growth, and cultural richness, while also examining the societal tensions and debates it has ignited.

Moreover, the chapter scrutinizes the current discourse on immigration policies, their implications on America's workforce, innovation, and global competitiveness. It navigates through the narratives surrounding immigration reform, border security, and the ethical dimensions of migration governance.

Diversity within American society is a defining characteristic, yet it also presents challenges and opportunities for forging a unified national identity. The chapter explores how notions of identity and inclusivity influence America's projection of itself globally and its ability to navigate international relations in an interconnected world.

Furthermore, the chapter examines the impact of immigration and diversity on soft power, cultural diplomacy, and America's ability to attract global talent and maintain a competitive edge.

By dissecting these intricate intersections between immigration, diversity, and national identity, this chapter aims to evaluate their implications for America's global standing, societal cohesion, and the strategies needed to leverage diversity as a strength in an increasingly interconnected world.

CHAPTER 10:
GLOBAL ALLIANCES AND DIPLOMATIC RELATIONS

In an interdependent world, global alliances and diplomatic relations are pivotal in shaping a nation's influence and navigating complex international challenges. This chapter delves into America's historical alliances, evolving diplomatic strategies, and their impact on its global standing.

The United States has traditionally cultivated robust alliances across the globe, fostering strategic partnerships that have shaped geopolitical landscapes. This chapter traces the historical evolution of these alliances, examining their significance in promoting shared values, security cooperation, and economic interdependence.

However, the global geopolitical landscape is undergoing shifts. This chapter scrutinizes the recalibration of America's alliances amidst changing power dynamics, emerging threats, and evolving global priorities. It delves into the challenges of maintaining and revitalizing existing alliances while forging new partnerships that reflect contemporary geopolitical realities.

Moreover, the chapter navigates through the nuances of diplomatic relations, assessing the efficacy of American diplomatic efforts in addressing transnational issues such as terrorism, cybersecurity, and pandemics. It explores the role of diplomacy in conflict resolution, peacebuilding, and fostering international cooperation.

The rise of multilateral forums and the dynamics of great power competition present both opportunities and challenges for American diplomacy. This chapter evaluates the nation's role in these forums, analyzing the effectiveness of multilateral approaches in addressing global challenges.

Through an in-depth analysis, this chapter aims to dissect the complexities of global alliances, diplomatic strategies, and their implications for America's global leadership, emphasizing the need for adaptive diplomatic approaches in a rapidly changing world.

CHAPTER 11: THE ROLE OF LEADERSHIP IN SHAPING GLOBAL INFLUENCE

Leadership plays a pivotal role in defining a nation's global influence and its ability to navigate a rapidly changing world. This chapter examines the significance of leadership styles, strategies, and individual leaders in shaping America's global standing.

Throughout history, visionary leadership has often been a catalyst for America's global initiatives, shaping policies, and fostering international cooperation. This chapter delves into the impact of leadership qualities such as diplomacy, vision, and adaptability on America's global influence.

The chapter scrutinizes the evolving leadership approaches across different administrations and their implications for foreign policy, alliances, and international engagements. It analyzes the continuity and shifts in America's leadership strategies, emphasizing the importance of consistency and adaptability in maintaining global leadership.

Moreover, the chapter explores the role of leadership in fostering global consensus on pressing issues like climate change, global health crises, and economic cooperation. It evaluates the influence of leadership in shaping narratives, fostering trust, and projecting soft power on the global stage.

Additionally, the chapter delves into the interconnectedness between domestic leadership stability and global influence. It assesses how internal political stability, governance, and domestic policies impact America's credibility and effectiveness in international affairs.

Through a comprehensive analysis, this chapter aims to dissect the multifaceted role of leadership in shaping America's global influence, highlighting the significance of strategic leadership decisions in navigating the complexities of an interconnected world.

CHAPTER 12: ECONOMIC POWERHOUSES BEYOND THE WEST

The landscape of economic power is witnessing a transformative shift as emerging economies, predominantly beyond the Western hemisphere, ascend to global prominence. This chapter delves into the rise of economic powerhouses outside the traditional Western spheres and their impact on the global economic order.

Nations like China, India, Brazil, and others are redefining economic dynamics, boasting rapid growth rates, expanding markets, and significant influence in global trade. This chapter scrutinizes the economic strategies, innovations, and investments driving their ascent as formidable economic forces.

Moreover, the chapter examines the interplay between these rising economic powers and the established Western economies, analyzing the implications of their growth on global trade patterns, investment flows, and economic alliances.

The Belt and Road Initiative, China's technological advancements, India's burgeoning tech industry, and Brazil's role in regional economic integration serve as case studies for understanding the strategies employed by these emerging economic giants.

Furthermore, the chapter navigates through the geopolitical implications of these economic shifts, evaluating how the rise of non-Western economic powerhouses impacts global governance structures, financial institutions, and the balance of economic influence.

The emergence of alternative economic models, regional trade agreements, and investment initiatives spearheaded by these nations challenges the traditional dominance of Western-centric economic frameworks.

By dissecting these economic transformations, this chapter aims to explore the rise of economic powerhouses beyond the West, assess their implications for the global economic landscape, and contemplate the strategies required to navigate a multipolar economic order.

CHAPTER 13:
THE IMPACT OF PANDEMICS AND GLOBAL CRISES

Pandemics and global crises have historically served as catalysts for significant shifts in the geopolitical landscape, reshaping societies, economies, and international relations. This chapter delves into the profound impact of pandemics and global crises, examining their implications for America's global position.

The COVID-19 pandemic serves as a poignant case study, highlighting the vulnerabilities exposed within global systems. This chapter scrutinizes how pandemics disrupt economic structures, strain healthcare systems, and reshape social norms, posing unprecedented challenges to global governance.

Moreover, the chapter explores the implications of such crises on international cooperation, alliances, and diplomatic relations. It evaluates how nations collaborate or compete in addressing shared challenges during crises, assessing the impact on global solidarity and trust.

Furthermore, the economic fallout, supply chain disruptions, and shifts in global priorities brought about by pandemics and global crises prompt reevaluations of resilience and preparedness strategies. This chapter navigates through the lessons learned and the adaptations required for nations, including the United States, to navigate future crises.

Additionally, the chapter analyzes the role of science, technology, and international collaboration in pandemic response efforts, emphasizing the significance of coordinated global action in mitigating the impact of such crises.

By dissecting the multifaceted repercussions of pandemics and global crises, this chapter aims to assess their lasting impact on America's global positioning, resilience, and strategies necessary to navigate an increasingly unpredictable world fraught with potential crises.

CHAPTER 14: SHIFTING NARRATIVES AND THE PERCEPTION OF POWER

Narratives wield immense influence in shaping perceptions of a nation's power and influence on the global stage. This chapter delves into the evolving narratives surrounding America's global role, assessing their impact on its perceived power and international standing.

Over time, narratives about America's leadership, values, and global contributions have undergone transformations. This chapter scrutinizes the factors contributing to these shifts in narratives, including geopolitical changes, socio-economic developments, and evolving cultural dynamics.

The role of media, digital platforms, and public diplomacy in shaping these narratives is a key focus. It analyzes how storytelling, information dissemination, and public discourse influence global perceptions of America's power, ideals, and role in global affairs.

Moreover, the chapter explores the influence of competing

narratives propagated by other global actors, examining how they challenge or complement America's narratives and influence global perceptions of power dynamics.

The intersectionality of narratives with issues like democracy, human rights, and social justice is also examined. It evaluates how these narratives impact America's soft power, moral authority, and its ability to galvanize international support for its initiatives.

Additionally, the chapter navigates through the role of historical legacies, cultural diplomacy, and public engagement in shaping narratives that resonate globally, projecting an image of America's values and aspirations.

Through a nuanced analysis, this chapter aims to dissect the complexities of shifting narratives and their profound implications for America's perceived power, global influence, and the strategies required to navigate and shape these evolving perceptions.

CHAPTER 15: THE FUTURE OF AMERICA'S GLOBAL POSITIONING

The future of America's global positioning is at a critical juncture, shaped by a confluence of evolving factors and global dynamics. This chapter engages in forecasting and analysis to envision potential trajectories and challenges that may influence America's global role in the years to come.

The evolving geopolitical landscape, economic transformations, technological advancements, and socio-political shifts present both opportunities and challenges for America's global standing. This chapter evaluates potential scenarios and trends that could shape the nation's role in the international arena.

Examining the impact of ongoing trends, such as multipolar power dynamics, technological disruptions, and global governance changes, the chapter aims to forecast potential implications for America's leadership position.

Moreover, it scrutinizes the role of adaptive policies, diplomatic strategies, and innovation in steering America's trajectory in an increasingly interconnected world.

Environmental sustainability, socio-cultural shifts, and demographic changes are also considered as pivotal factors influencing America's future global positioning.

Furthermore, the chapter explores the implications of internal challenges, such as political polarization, social disparities, and economic vulnerabilities, on America's ability to sustain global leadership and navigate emerging global challenges.

Through an interdisciplinary approach, drawing insights from geopolitics, economics, technology, and societal trends, this chapter aims to provide a comprehensive exploration of potential scenarios and the dynamics that could shape the future landscape of America's global positioning.

CHAPTER 16: TECHNOLOGICAL SOVEREIGNTY AND SECURITY CONCERNS

The concept of technological sovereignty has emerged as a critical aspect in the contemporary global landscape, encompassing issues of data control, technological independence, and national security. This chapter delves into the intricate intersections between technological sovereignty and the evolving security concerns faced by nations, including the United States.

Technological advancements have intertwined deeply with national security, raising questions about the control and protection of critical technologies, data, and infrastructure. The chapter navigates through the challenges posed by reliance on foreign technologies and the pursuit of self-reliance in strategic sectors.

Furthermore, the chapter scrutinizes the implications of emerging technologies such as 5G networks, quantum computing, and AI on national security paradigms. It evaluates the risks of technological dependencies and the strategies nations employ to safeguard against cyber threats, espionage, and technological vulnerabilities.

The discourse around data privacy, surveillance, and the balance between security and civil liberties is also explored within the context of technological sovereignty. The chapter assesses how regulations, policies, and international collaborations shape the technological landscape and influence security dynamics.

Additionally, the chapter examines the evolving role of tech corporations, their global reach, and their implications for national security interests. It also addresses the ethical considerations associated with technological development and their impact on sovereignty and security.

By delving into these complexities, the chapter aims to provide insights into the challenges and opportunities inherent in technological sovereignty, emphasizing its profound implications for national security strategies and the evolving global order.

CHAPTER 17: THE GEOECONOMICS OF RESOURCE COMPETITION

Resource competition has evolved into a central facet of global geopolitics, influencing economic strategies, alliances, and power dynamics. This chapter explores the intricate interplay between geoeconomics and the competition for crucial resources, examining its implications for America's global position.

Scarce resources, including energy reserves, rare minerals, water, and arable land, have become focal points in the geopolitical landscape. The chapter scrutinizes how nations vie for access, control, and influence over these resources, shaping economic policies and strategic alliances.

Furthermore, it delves into the geopolitical ramifications of resource-rich regions, analyzing how control or disputes over these areas influence global power dynamics and regional stability.

The chapter navigates through the strategies employed by nations to secure resource supplies, including diplomatic engagements, trade agreements, and investments in resource-rich regions. It also assesses the implications of resource competition on economic interdependence and the potential for conflicts arising from resource scarcity.

Additionally, the chapter addresses the environmental implications of resource extraction and the quest for sustainability in managing resource competition. It examines how shifts in global attitudes towards environmental conservation impact resource strategies and international relations.

Moreover, emerging renewable energy technologies, circular economy concepts, and advancements in resource management strategies are evaluated within the context of altering geoeconomic landscapes.

By dissecting the complexities of resource competition, this chapter aims to offer insights into its profound impact on geopolitical strategies, economic alliances, and the evolving global order, providing a nuanced perspective on its implications for America's global positioning.

CHAPTER 18: CULTURAL DIPLOMACY IN A DIGITAL AGE

In an era of rapid globalization and digital interconnectedness, cultural diplomacy has taken on a new dimension, wielding significant influence in shaping international relations. This chapter explores the evolving landscape of cultural diplomacy in the digital age and its implications for America's global engagement.

Cultural diplomacy, once primarily conducted through traditional channels such as art exhibitions, exchange programs, and cultural events, has now expanded into the digital realm. The chapter examines how social media, digital platforms, and virtual experiences are reshaping the way nations project their cultural narratives globally.

Moreover, it delves into the role of cultural exchange in fostering mutual understanding, bridging divides, and building soft power. The chapter scrutinizes how digital connectivity facilitates cross-cultural interactions, enabling nations, including the United States, to showcase their cultural diversity and values to a global audience.

Furthermore, the chapter navigates through the challenges and opportunities presented by digital cultural diplomacy, including issues of cultural authenticity, censorship, and the potential for misinformation or cultural stereotypes in the digital sphere.

The impact of cultural diplomacy on public perceptions, national branding, and international relations is also examined. It assesses how cultural narratives, storytelling, and cultural exchanges influence global perceptions of nations and their policies.

Additionally, the chapter evaluates the role of cultural diplomacy in addressing global challenges such as xenophobia, extremism, and fostering intercultural dialogue for peaceful coexistence in a diverse world.

By analyzing the complexities of cultural diplomacy in the digital age, this chapter aims to shed light on its significance as a tool for global engagement, its impact on America's image and influence, and the strategies required to navigate this evolving landscape effectively.

CHAPTER 19: HUMANITARIAN INTERVENTIONS AND GLOBAL RESPONSIBILITY

Humanitarian interventions play a pivotal role in addressing crises, protecting vulnerable populations, and upholding global responsibility. This chapter delves into the complexities surrounding humanitarian interventions and their implications for America's global role and moral standing.

Amidst conflicts, natural disasters, and humanitarian crises, the international community often faces dilemmas about when and how to intervene. The chapter examines the moral imperatives, legal frameworks, and ethical considerations guiding humanitarian interventions.

Moreover, it scrutinizes the role of America and other global actors in leading or participating in humanitarian interventions, assessing the impact of such actions on international cooperation, stability, and the protection of human rights.

The chapter navigates through the challenges and controversies associated with humanitarian interventions, including debates over sovereignty, intervention legitimacy, and the unintended consequences of interventionist policies.

Furthermore, it addresses the complexities of providing humanitarian aid, the role of non-governmental organizations (NGOs), and the changing dynamics of humanitarian assistance in conflict zones and fragile states.

Additionally, the chapter evaluates the evolving concept of the Responsibility to Protect (R2P) and its implications for global governance, emphasizing the balance between sovereignty and the international community's duty to protect civilians from atrocities.

By analyzing these intricate facets of humanitarian interventions, this chapter aims to assess their role in shaping America's global responsibilities, moral obligations, and the strategies needed to navigate the complexities of intervening in humanitarian crises while upholding global ethical standards.

CHAPTER 20: THE ROLE OF EDUCATION IN GLOBAL COMPETITIVENESS

Education serves as a cornerstone for national development and global competitiveness. This chapter delves into the pivotal role of education in shaping a nation's workforce, innovation, and international standing, focusing on its implications for America's global competitiveness.

Quality education systems foster skilled workforces, innovation, and economic growth. The chapter examines how education policies and reforms influence a nation's ability to adapt to rapid technological changes and compete in the global economy.

Moreover, it explores the significance of higher education institutions, research centers, and vocational training programs in driving innovation and nurturing talent capable of addressing complex global challenges.

The chapter navigates through the role of educational diplomacy, student exchanges, and international collaborations in fostering cultural understanding, global partnerships, and soft power projection for nations, including the United States.

Additionally, it addresses the challenges of education inequality, access to quality education, and the digital divide, which impact a nation's capacity to cultivate a competitive workforce and innovative thinkers.

Furthermore, it evaluates emerging trends in education, including online learning, skills-based education, and lifelong learning initiatives, and their potential to reshape educational landscapes and enhance global competitiveness.

By scrutinizing the nexus between education and global competitiveness, this chapter aims to underscore the importance of education as a catalyst for nations to maintain and improve their competitive edge in an ever-evolving global landscape.

CHAPTER 21: EVOLVING STRATEGIES IN CYBERSECURITY AND DIGITAL WARFARE

In an interconnected world, cybersecurity and digital warfare have emerged as critical domains shaping national security and global stability. This chapter delves into the complexities of these evolving strategies, examining their significance for America's defense and its role in maintaining global security.

Cyber threats pose multifaceted challenges, ranging from state-sponsored cyberattacks to cybercrime and digital espionage. The chapter scrutinizes how nations, including the United States, are adapting their defense strategies to counter these evolving threats.

Moreover, it explores the interconnectedness between cybersecurity and critical infrastructure, evaluating the vulnerabilities and implications of cyberattacks on essential systems such as energy, finance, and healthcare.

The chapter navigates through the role of international norms, agreements, and collaborations in establishing cybersecurity frameworks and mitigating global cyber risks. It also addresses the ethical considerations and the evolving legal landscape surrounding cyber warfare and digital espionage.

Furthermore, it delves into the concept of offensive cyber capabilities and their role in deterrence strategies, as well as the challenges of attribution and establishing rules of engagement in cyberspace.

Additionally, the chapter examines the intersection between artificial intelligence, quantum computing, and cybersecurity, assessing how technological advancements shape the future of digital warfare.

By dissecting these intricate domains, this chapter aims to provide insights into the complexities of cybersecurity and digital warfare, emphasizing the importance of adaptive strategies and international cooperation in safeguarding national interests and global stability in an increasingly digitized world.

CHAPTER 22: GENDER DYNAMICS AND GLOBAL LEADERSHIP

The dynamics of gender play a significant but often overlooked role in shaping global leadership and governance. This chapter explores the complexities surrounding gender dynamics and their implications for global leadership, including America's role in promoting gender equality on the global stage.

Historically, leadership positions have been predominantly occupied by men, but there's a growing recognition of the value of diverse perspectives in leadership. The chapter scrutinizes the impact of gender diversity in leadership roles, examining how it influences decision-making, policy formulation, and international relations.

Moreover, it navigates through the challenges faced by women in accessing leadership positions, gender biases, and cultural barriers that hinder their advancement in politics, diplomacy, and corporate leadership.

The chapter also assesses the importance of inclusive leadership in fostering innovation, addressing global challenges, and promoting social and economic development.

Furthermore, it explores the role of women leaders in diplomacy, peace negotiations, and conflict resolution, highlighting their unique contributions and the impact of their participation on global agendas.

Additionally, the chapter addresses initiatives, policies, and international frameworks aimed at promoting gender equality and women's empowerment, emphasizing the significance of these efforts in creating more equitable and effective global leadership structures.

By dissecting these gender dynamics, this chapter aims to underscore the importance of diverse leadership in global governance, the challenges hindering gender parity, and the strategies required to promote inclusivity and equality in global leadership roles.

CHAPTER 23:
THE IMPACT OF URBANIZATION ON GLOBAL DYNAMICS

Urbanization stands as a transformative force, shaping societies, economies, and global dynamics. This chapter delves into the profound impact of urbanization on various facets of global affairs and its implications for America's role in an increasingly urbanized world.

Rapid urbanization has led to the concentration of populations, resources, and economic activities in cities. The chapter examines how this trend influences consumption patterns, resource demands, and environmental sustainability on a global scale.

Moreover, it navigates through the socioeconomic implications of urbanization, including issues of inequality, migration, and social cohesion. It explores the challenges and opportunities arising from the urban-rural divide and its influence on global economic disparities.

The chapter scrutinizes the role of cities as centers of innovation, culture, and economic growth, analyzing their contributions to global competitiveness, technological advancements, and international trade.

Furthermore, it addresses the environmental footprint of urbanization, discussing initiatives for sustainable urban development, resilient infrastructure, and the mitigation of urban challenges such as pollution, congestion, and housing.

Additionally, it evaluates the political significance of cities in global governance, exploring networks of global cities and their growing influence on international policies and cooperation.

By dissecting the multifaceted impacts of urbanization, this chapter aims to offer insights into the far-reaching consequences of global urbanization trends, their implications for America's global engagements, and the strategies necessary to harness the potential of urban centers for sustainable global development.

CHAPTER 24: SOFT POWER IN INTERNATIONAL RELATIONS: REASSESSING INFLUENCE

Soft power, the ability to shape the preferences of others through attraction and persuasion rather than coercion, holds substantial sway in international relations. This chapter undertakes a reassessment of soft power dynamics, examining their significance for nations, including the United States, in influencing global affairs.

The chapter begins by defining and contextualizing soft power, exploring its components such as culture, diplomacy, education, and values. It scrutinizes how nations utilize soft power to build alliances, promote their agendas, and enhance their global influence.

Moreover, it navigates through the changing landscape of soft power in the digital era, analyzing how social media, information dissemination, and cultural exports redefine the tools and reach of soft power.

The chapter delves into case studies highlighting successful instances of soft power utilization and the factors contributing to their effectiveness in influencing global perceptions and policies.

Additionally, it addresses the ethical dimensions of soft power, considering issues such as cultural imperialism, authenticity, and the potential for manipulation in shaping narratives and perceptions.

Furthermore, it evaluates the comparative advantages and limitations of soft power vis-à-vis hard power in achieving foreign policy objectives, emphasizing the importance of a balanced approach in a rapidly evolving global context.

By dissecting the evolving dynamics of soft power, this chapter aims to offer insights into its nuances, impact, and strategic implications for nations aspiring to enhance their global influence in contemporary international relations.

CHAPTER 25: ETHICAL DIMENSIONS OF ARTIFICIAL INTELLIGENCE AND ROBOTICS

Artificial Intelligence (AI) and robotics hold immense promise for innovation and progress, yet their ethical implications pose profound questions for societies worldwide. This chapter delves into the ethical dimensions surrounding AI and robotics, exploring their implications for society, governance, and global norms.

The chapter begins by examining the ethical considerations inherent in AI development, including issues of bias, transparency, and accountability in algorithmic decision-making processes. It navigates through the challenges of ensuring AI systems operate ethically and align with societal values.

Moreover, it scrutinizes the implications of AI and robotics on labor markets, job displacement, and the ethical responsibilities of industries and governments in managing these transitions responsibly.

Furthermore, the chapter explores the ethical dilemmas in the use of AI in sensitive domains like healthcare, law enforcement, and warfare, analyzing the potential risks and benefits and the need for ethical guidelines to govern their application.

Additionally, it addresses the moral considerations surrounding the development of autonomous systems, examining the implications of delegating decisions to AI and robotics in contexts such as self-driving cars or autonomous weapons.

The chapter also delves into global perspectives on AI ethics, exploring efforts to establish international norms and standards for the responsible development and use of AI and robotics.

By dissecting the ethical complexities of AI and robotics, this chapter aims to provide insights into the moral considerations shaping their deployment, the importance of ethical frameworks in governance, and the implications of ethical choices for the global adoption of these technologies.

CHAPTER 26: MIGRATION PATTERNS AND SOCIOECONOMIC TRANSFORMATIONS

Migration stands as a powerful driver of socioeconomic change, shaping cultures, economies, and global dynamics. This chapter delves into the intricate relationship between migration patterns and their profound implications for socioeconomic transformations worldwide, including their impact on America's global outlook.

The chapter begins by examining diverse migration patterns, including forced displacement, economic migration, and refugee flows. It navigates through the factors influencing migration, such as conflict, economic opportunities, environmental changes, and political instability.

Moreover, it scrutinizes the socio-economic contributions of migrants to both origin and destination countries, assessing their role in fostering innovation, cultural diversity, and economic growth.

The chapter explores the challenges faced by migrants, including issues of integration, discrimination, and access to basic rights and services. It addresses the ethical dimensions of migration policies, emphasizing the importance of humanitarian approaches in managing migration crises.

Furthermore, it evaluates the impact of migration on labor markets, demographics, and social cohesion in both sending and receiving countries, analyzing how these transformations influence global economies and societies.

Additionally, it addresses the intersectionality of migration with global challenges, such as climate change-induced migration, human trafficking, and the implications of irregular migration on international security.

By dissecting these migration dynamics, this chapter aims to provide insights into the multifaceted impact of migration on global socio-economic landscapes, emphasizing the importance of inclusive policies and international cooperation to address the challenges and harness the potential of migration for positive socioeconomic transformations.

CHAPTER 27: RELIGIOUS INFLUENCE IN GEOPOLITICS AND INTERNATIONAL RELATIONS

The interplay between religion and geopolitics remains a significant force shaping global affairs and international relations. This chapter delves into the multifaceted influence of religion on geopolitics, exploring its implications for global dynamics and America's role in navigating religious diversity on the global stage.

Religious beliefs, ideologies, and identities often intersect with political agendas and international relations. The chapter navigates through the role of religion in shaping geopolitical alliances, conflicts, and regional power dynamics across different parts of the world.

Moreover, it scrutinizes the influence of religious leaders, movements, and ideologies on global agendas, peace negotiations, and conflict resolution, analyzing how they impact international cooperation and security.

The chapter delves into the complexities of religious diversity, examining how religious pluralism shapes societies, governance, and cultural identities, emphasizing the need for religious tolerance and dialogue in fostering global peace.

Furthermore, it addresses the challenges posed by religious extremism, terrorism, and sectarian conflicts, exploring how these issues disrupt geopolitical stability and pose threats to global security.

Additionally, it evaluates the role of religious diplomacy and interfaith dialogue in fostering mutual understanding, promoting tolerance, and mitigating religious-based conflicts in an increasingly interconnected world.

By dissecting the influence of religion in geopolitics and international relations, this chapter aims to offer insights into the complexities of religious dynamics, their impact on global affairs, and the strategies necessary to navigate religious diversity while promoting global stability and cooperation.

CHAPTER 28:
HEALTH DIPLOMACY
AND PANDEMIC
PREPAREDNESS

Health diplomacy and pandemic preparedness have emerged as critical components of global governance and international relations. This chapter delves into the significance of health diplomacy in managing global health crises, including pandemics, and its implications for international cooperation, with a focus on America's role in global health security.

The chapter begins by examining the concept of health diplomacy, emphasizing the role of nations in collaborating to address transnational health challenges. It navigates through the historical evolution of global health governance and the frameworks established for pandemic preparedness and response.

Moreover, it scrutinizes the impact of health crises, especially pandemics like COVID-19, on international relations, economies, and global stability. It assesses the effectiveness of multilateral efforts and international organizations in coordinating responses to health emergencies.

The chapter explores the role of scientific cooperation, data sharing, and vaccine diplomacy in managing global health threats. It addresses the ethical dimensions of equitable access to healthcare and vaccines, emphasizing the need for inclusive and fair distribution mechanisms.

Furthermore, it evaluates the intersection between health security and national security, analyzing how health crises can affect geopolitics, economic stability, and social cohesion.

Additionally, it navigates through the lessons learned from past health crises, emphasizing the necessity for robust pandemic preparedness strategies, resilient healthcare systems, and international collaboration to mitigate future health threats.

By dissecting health diplomacy and pandemic preparedness, this chapter aims to underscore their critical role in global governance, their implications for America's global engagements, and the strategies required for effective collaboration in safeguarding global health security.

CHAPTER 29: CLIMATE CHANGE RESILIENCE AND ADAPTATION STRATEGIES

Climate change stands as a defining challenge of the 21st century, requiring global cooperation and concerted efforts to mitigate its impacts. This chapter delves into the imperative for climate change resilience and adaptation strategies, examining their significance for nations, including the United States, and their role in shaping global sustainability.

The chapter begins by addressing the repercussions of climate change, including rising temperatures, extreme weather events, sea-level rise, and ecological disruptions. It navigates through the impact of these changes on societies, economies, and global stability.

Moreover, it scrutinizes the necessity for resilience and adaptation strategies to mitigate the adverse effects of climate change. It examines initiatives undertaken by nations, communities, and international organizations to build resilience in vulnerable regions and develop adaptive measures.

The chapter explores the role of innovative technologies, renewable energy, and sustainable practices in fostering climate resilience. It assesses how investments in climate adaptation can create opportunities for economic growth and foster sustainable development.

Furthermore, it evaluates the importance of international cooperation, climate agreements, and collective action in addressing climate change challenges. It examines the effectiveness of global frameworks like the Paris Agreement in driving climate action.

Additionally, it navigates through the ethical considerations of climate change, emphasizing the responsibilities of nations to mitigate their carbon footprint and assist vulnerable communities in adapting to climate-related risks.

By dissecting climate change resilience and adaptation strategies, this chapter aims to underscore their critical importance in global sustainability efforts, their implications for America's environmental policies, and the necessity for collaborative approaches to combat climate change on a global scale.

CHAPTER 30: FUTURE TRENDS IN INTERNATIONAL TRADE AND ECONOMIC ALLIANCES

The landscape of international trade and economic alliances is continuously evolving, influenced by technological advancements, geopolitical shifts, and changing global dynamics. This chapter delves into the anticipated trends shaping the future of international trade and economic alliances, examining their implications for global economies, including the role of the United States.

The chapter begins by analyzing the impact of technological innovations, such as digitalization, automation, and the Internet of Things (IoT), on global trade patterns. It navigates through the transformation of supply chains, e-commerce, and digital trade, exploring their influence on global economic alliances.

Moreover, it scrutinizes the regionalization and diversification of trade alliances, assessing the emergence of new economic blocs and trade agreements. It examines the potential implications of these shifts on global economic power dynamics and trade partnerships.

The chapter explores the interplay between trade policies, geopolitical tensions, and the rise of protectionism, analyzing how these factors influence international trade agreements and economic cooperation.

Furthermore, it evaluates the impact of sustainability and environmental considerations on trade policies, exploring how initiatives for green economies and circular trade models shape future economic alliances.

Additionally, it addresses the role of multilateral organizations, such as the World Trade Organization (WTO), in shaping future trade norms, regulations, and dispute resolution mechanisms.

By dissecting the anticipated trends in international trade and economic alliances, this chapter aims to provide insights into the evolving landscape of global trade dynamics, their implications for America's economic engagements, and the strategies required to adapt to and leverage these trends for sustainable economic growth.

CHAPTER 31: DIGITAL CURRENCIES AND THE FUTURE OF FINANCIAL SYSTEMS

Digital currencies, particularly cryptocurrencies like Bitcoin and Ethereum, are reshaping the landscape of traditional financial systems. This chapter explores the evolution of digital currencies and their profound implications for the future of financial systems worldwide.

The chapter begins by tracing the origins of digital currencies, highlighting their decentralized nature, blockchain technology, and the growing adoption of cryptocurrencies as alternative assets.

Moreover, it scrutinizes the impact of digital currencies on traditional banking and financial institutions, exploring how these innovations challenge conventional monetary systems and payment infrastructures.

The chapter navigates through the potential benefits and risks associated with digital currencies, examining their role in financial inclusion, cross-border transactions, and the democratization of finance.

Furthermore, it evaluates the regulatory challenges and policy considerations surrounding digital currencies, addressing issues of security, consumer protection, and their integration into existing financial frameworks.

Additionally, it delves into the emergence of central bank digital currencies (CBDCs) and their implications for monetary policies, financial stability, and the global economic order.

By dissecting the intricacies of digital currencies, this chapter aims to provide insights into their transformative potential, the challenges they pose to traditional financial systems, and the implications for the future of global finance and monetary governance.

CHAPTER 32: IMPACT OF DEMOGRAPHIC SHIFTS ON GLOBAL ECONOMIES

Demographic shifts, including changes in population size, age distribution, and migration patterns, wield profound influence on global economies. This chapter explores the multifaceted impact of these demographic changes and their implications for economies worldwide.

The chapter begins by analyzing the effects of aging populations in some regions and youthful demographics in others. It navigates through how these demographic changes influence labor markets, productivity, and economic growth trajectories.

Moreover, it scrutinizes the implications of changing demographics on social welfare systems, healthcare expenditures, and pension schemes, addressing the challenges and opportunities posed by shifting age structures.

The chapter explores the impact of migration on labor forces, consumption patterns, and cultural dynamics, evaluating how migration trends reshape economies and contribute to diversity in various regions.

Furthermore, it assesses the economic consequences of demographic transitions, such as urbanization, changing family structures, and their influence on consumer behaviors and market demands.

Additionally, it delves into the intersections between demographics, technology adoption, and skill demands in labor markets, analyzing how these factors shape future economic landscapes.

By dissecting the intricate linkages between demographic shifts and global economies, this chapter aims to provide insights into their far-reaching impacts, their implications for economic policies, and the strategies necessary to leverage demographic changes for sustainable economic development.

CHAPTER 33: GEOPOLITICAL RAMIFICATIONS OF ENERGY TRANSITION

The transition from traditional fossil fuels to renewable energy sources is reshaping global geopolitics and power dynamics. This chapter delves into the geopolitical implications stemming from this energy transition and its impact on international relations.

The chapter begins by exploring the shifting dynamics of energy production and consumption, emphasizing the rise of renewable energy sources like solar, wind, and hydroelectric power. It navigates through how this transition affects the geopolitical landscape by altering energy dependencies and global energy markets.

Moreover, it scrutinizes the impact of energy transition on the influence and strategies of energy-rich nations, highlighting how traditional oil-producing countries are adapting to the changing energy paradigm.

The chapter evaluates the role of renewable energy technologies in fostering energy independence among nations, potentially reshaping alliances and reducing conflicts related to energy resources.

Furthermore, it examines the interplay between energy transition, climate diplomacy, and international cooperation, emphasizing the collaborative efforts needed to address climate change and achieve sustainable energy goals.

Additionally, it addresses the challenges and opportunities arising from the shift to renewable energy, including geopolitical tensions over access to critical minerals for renewable technologies and the geopolitical implications of a more decentralized energy infrastructure.

By dissecting the geopolitical ramifications of the energy transition, this chapter aims to provide insights into the reshaping of global power dynamics, the potential for geopolitical conflicts, and the necessity for cooperative strategies in navigating the evolving energy landscape.

CHAPTER 34: ARTIFICIAL INTELLIGENCE IN GOVERNANCE AND PUBLIC SERVICES

The integration of artificial intelligence (AI) in governance and public services heralds a transformative era in administration and citizen services. This chapter explores the burgeoning impact of AI applications in reshaping governance structures and public service delivery.

The chapter begins by examining the role of AI in enhancing government efficiency through predictive analytics, data-driven decision-making, and streamlining administrative processes.

Moreover, it scrutinizes AI's potential in optimizing public services, such as healthcare, transportation, education, and urban planning, by improving service delivery, resource allocation, and citizen engagement.

The chapter navigates through the ethical considerations in deploying AI in governance, addressing issues of transparency, accountability, and biases in automated decision-making systems.

Furthermore, it evaluates the challenges and opportunities in the adoption of AI, including concerns related to data privacy, cybersecurity, and the need for upskilling public sector employees to harness AI capabilities effectively.

Additionally, it explores the potential impact of AI-driven smart cities, digital governments, and e-governance initiatives in fostering inclusive and responsive governance structures.

By dissecting the integration of AI in governance and public services, this chapter aims to provide insights into the transformative potential of AI, the challenges inherent in its deployment, and the strategies necessary for leveraging AI for effective and equitable public administration.

CHAPTER 35: URBAN DEVELOPMENT AND SUSTAINABLE INFRASTRUCTURE

Urban development is at the forefront of global transformations, necessitating sustainable infrastructure to meet the demands of burgeoning populations. This chapter explores the critical role of sustainable infrastructure in urban development and its implications for global sustainability.

The chapter begins by analyzing the challenges posed by rapid urbanization, including the strain on existing infrastructure, increased energy consumption, and environmental degradation.

Moreover, it scrutinizes the concept of sustainable infrastructure, encompassing resilient transportation systems, green buildings, renewable energy sources, and efficient waste management, emphasizing their role in creating livable and sustainable cities.

The chapter navigates through the innovative approaches and technologies driving sustainable urban development, including smart city initiatives, circular economy principles, and nature-based solutions for urban challenges.

Furthermore, it evaluates the economic, environmental, and social benefits of investing in sustainable infrastructure, emphasizing its capacity to foster economic growth, mitigate climate change impacts, and improve the quality of life for urban residents.

Additionally, it addresses the role of public-private partnerships, international collaborations, and policy frameworks in promoting sustainable urban development on a global scale.

By dissecting the nexus between urban development and sustainable infrastructure, this chapter aims to underscore the importance of investing in sustainable urbanization, its implications for global sustainability goals, and the strategies necessary for building resilient and inclusive cities for the future.

CHAPTER 36:
EVOLUTION OF SPACE EXPLORATION AND ITS SOCIOECONOMIC IMPACTS

Space exploration has transcended boundaries, contributing to scientific advancements and influencing socioeconomic landscapes. This chapter delves into the evolutionary trajectory of space exploration and its far-reaching impacts on societies and economies worldwide.

The chapter begins by tracing the historical milestones of space exploration, from early missions to the Moon to the advent of space stations and interplanetary missions.

Moreover, it scrutinizes the socioeconomic implications of space exploration, including technological innovations that originated from space programs, such as satellite technology, GPS systems, and advancements in materials science and healthcare.

The chapter navigates through the economic impacts of space endeavors, including the emergence of commercial space industries, the space tourism sector, and the development of new markets driven by space-related technologies.

Furthermore, it evaluates the societal impacts of space exploration, analyzing how space missions inspire STEM education, foster international collaborations, and influence cultural perceptions of human potential and exploration.

Additionally, it addresses the challenges and opportunities in expanding space exploration efforts, including sustainability concerns, space debris management, and ethical considerations in future space endeavors.

By dissecting the evolution of space exploration and its socioeconomic impacts, this chapter aims to provide insights into the transformative influence of space missions on technological innovation, economic growth, and societal aspirations, while highlighting the challenges and opportunities in the pursuit of space exploration.

CHAPTER 37: CULTURAL EXCHANGE IN THE DIGITAL ERA: REDEFINING BOUNDARIES

The digital era has revolutionized cultural exchange, reshaping how societies interact, share, and celebrate diversity. This chapter explores the transformative impact of digital platforms on cultural exchange and its role in redefining boundaries.

The chapter begins by examining how digital technologies have democratized cultural exchange, enabling instant connectivity across borders, fostering global conversations, and facilitating the sharing of diverse cultural expressions.

Moreover, it scrutinizes the role of social media, streaming platforms, and virtual experiences in bridging cultural gaps, promoting cross-cultural understanding, and amplifying voices from marginalized communities worldwide.

The chapter navigates through the challenges and opportunities presented by the digital era in preserving cultural heritage, addressing issues of cultural appropriation, and fostering inclusive platforms for cultural expression.

Furthermore, it evaluates the impact of digital cultural exchange on global perceptions, identities, and the evolution of cultural norms in an interconnected world.

Additionally, it addresses the role of governments, international organizations, and grassroots initiatives in leveraging digital platforms for fostering intercultural dialogue and preserving cultural diversity.

By dissecting cultural exchange in the digital era, this chapter aims to provide insights into its transformative potential, the challenges it poses to traditional notions of culture, and the opportunities for creating inclusive, interconnected societies through digital platforms.

CHAPTER 38: FUTURE OF WORK: AUTOMATION, GIG ECONOMY, AND SKILL SETS

The evolving landscape of work is undergoing profound transformations driven by automation, the rise of the gig economy, and shifting skill requirements. This chapter explores the future of work amidst these changes and their impact on employment dynamics and skill development.

The chapter begins by analyzing the implications of automation and artificial intelligence on job markets, industries, and the nature of work. It navigates through how technological advancements reshape job roles, emphasizing the importance of upskilling and reskilling for workforce adaptability.

Moreover, it scrutinizes the growth of the gig economy, freelance work, and remote employment, examining their influence on traditional employment structures, job security, and the work-life balance of individuals.

The chapter explores the significance of soft skills, creativity, and adaptability in the future job market, alongside the demand for technical expertise and digital literacy.

Furthermore, it evaluates the role of education and training systems in preparing individuals for the future workforce, emphasizing the need for agile learning models and lifelong skill development.

Additionally, it addresses the socio-economic impacts of these shifts, including income inequality, labor rights, and the need for updated policies to protect and support workers in this evolving work landscape.

By dissecting the future of work in light of automation, the gig economy, and changing skill demands, this chapter aims to provide insights into the challenges and opportunities for individuals, businesses, and policymakers in navigating the transforming nature of employment.

CHAPTER 39: GLOBAL HEALTH GOVERNANCE AND PANDEMIC PREVENTION

Global health governance stands as a critical framework for coordinating efforts to address public health crises and prevent future pandemics. This chapter delves into the significance of robust health governance systems and their role in pandemic prevention on a global scale.

The chapter begins by examining the structures and mechanisms of global health governance, emphasizing the roles of international organizations, agreements, and collaborations in coordinating responses to health emergencies.

Moreover, it scrutinizes the lessons learned from past pandemics, analyzing how these experiences have shaped global health policies and strategies for pandemic prevention and preparedness.

The chapter navigates through the challenges faced by global health governance structures, including funding gaps, access to vaccines and healthcare, and disparities in health outcomes among nations.

Furthermore, it evaluates the impact of interconnectedness and mobility on the spread of infectious diseases, emphasizing the need for coordinated international efforts in surveillance, early detection, and response to potential health threats.

Additionally, it addresses the ethical considerations and equity issues in access to healthcare and vaccines, advocating for inclusive strategies in global health governance.

By dissecting the landscape of global health governance and pandemic prevention, this chapter aims to provide insights into the necessity for collaborative and resilient health systems, the challenges hindering effective responses to health crises, and the strategies required for building a more prepared and responsive global health governance framework.

CHAPTER 40: SECURING FOOD SYSTEMS IN A CHANGING CLIMATE

The confluence of climate change and its impact on agriculture poses significant challenges to global food systems. This chapter explores the complexities of securing food systems amidst a changing climate and the measures necessary for resilience and sustainability.

The chapter begins by analyzing the effects of climate change on agricultural productivity, including shifts in weather patterns, water scarcity, and the increased frequency of extreme events like droughts and floods.

Moreover, it scrutinizes the vulnerability of food supply chains to climate-related disruptions, addressing issues of food insecurity, distribution challenges, and access to nutritious food in vulnerable regions.

The chapter navigates through innovative agricultural practices and technologies that promote climate resilience, such as precision farming, drought-resistant crops, and sustainable irrigation methods.

Furthermore, it evaluates the role of policy interventions, international collaborations, and investments in climate-smart agriculture to mitigate the adverse impacts of climate change on food systems.

Additionally, it addresses the importance of promoting biodiversity, preserving natural ecosystems, and reducing food waste as strategies to enhance the resilience of food systems.

By dissecting the challenges posed by climate change to food security and exploring potential solutions, this chapter aims to provide insights into building more resilient, sustainable, and adaptive food systems capable of withstanding the pressures of a changing climate.

CHAPTER 41:
INTELLECTUAL PROPERTY RIGHTS IN INNOVATION AND TECHNOLOGY

Intellectual property (IP) rights play a pivotal role in fostering innovation and technological advancements, shaping the modern landscape of progress. This chapter delves into the significance of IP rights in the realm of innovation and technology.

The chapter begins by examining the role of patents, copyrights, trademarks, and trade secrets in protecting inventions, creative works, and innovations. It navigates through their influence on incentivizing research, development, and creativity across various industries.

Moreover, it scrutinizes the challenges posed by the intersection of technology and IP rights, especially in areas like artificial intelligence, biotechnology, and digital content distribution, addressing issues of ownership, licensing, and fair use.

The chapter explores the impact of IP rights on market

competition, entrepreneurship, and market access, assessing their role in fostering a conducive environment for innovation while ensuring fair competition.

Furthermore, it evaluates the global landscape of IP rights, analyzing international agreements, treaties, and harmonization efforts aimed at balancing protection and access to innovations.

Additionally, it addresses the ethical dimensions of IP rights, discussing debates around access to essential medicines, open-source movements, and the balance between IP protection and the public interest.

By dissecting the complexities of intellectual property rights in innovation and technology, this chapter aims to provide insights into their multifaceted impacts, the challenges in adapting IP laws to technological advancements, and the implications for fostering a dynamic and innovative global environment.

CHAPTER 42: GEOECONOMIC IMPACT OF WATER SCARCITY AND MANAGEMENT

Water scarcity has emerged as a critical global challenge with multifaceted geoeconomic implications, influencing regions, economies, and international relations. This chapter explores the far-reaching geoeconomic impacts of water scarcity and the imperative for effective water management strategies.

The chapter begins by analyzing the geoeconomic consequences of water scarcity, addressing its impact on agriculture, industry, and human health, and the subsequent strain on economies and livelihoods.

Moreover, it scrutinizes the role of water in geopolitical tensions and conflicts, emphasizing the potential for water disputes to influence regional stability and international relations.

The chapter navigates through the economic implications of inadequate water management practices, including decreased agricultural productivity, increased water-related disasters, and rising costs for businesses and governments.

Furthermore, it evaluates the importance of sustainable water management practices, investment in water infrastructure, and technological innovations for mitigating water scarcity's economic burdens.

Additionally, it addresses the potential for international cooperation, transboundary water agreements, and collaborative approaches in managing water resources to foster regional stability and economic growth.

By dissecting the geoeconomic impacts of water scarcity and the significance of proactive water management strategies, this chapter aims to provide insights into the interconnectedness of water challenges with global economies, the potential for water-related conflicts, and the opportunities for collaborative solutions on a global scale.

CHAPTER 43:
EMERGING MARKETS AND INVESTMENT OPPORTUNITIES

Emerging markets present dynamic opportunities for investors seeking growth, diversification, and new avenues for capital deployment. This chapter explores the landscape of emerging markets, their characteristics, and the investment opportunities they offer.

The chapter begins by defining emerging markets, analyzing their economic fundamentals, growth prospects, and unique attributes that make them attractive destinations for investment.

Moreover, it scrutinizes the diverse sectors within emerging markets that offer investment potential, such as technology, renewable energy, consumer goods, and healthcare, assessing their growth trajectories and market dynamics.

The chapter navigates through the risks and challenges associated with investing in emerging markets, including political instability, regulatory uncertainties, and currency volatility, providing insights into risk mitigation strategies.

Furthermore, it evaluates the impact of globalization, trade agreements, and geopolitical shifts on the attractiveness of emerging markets for investors, emphasizing the importance of understanding local contexts and market nuances.

Additionally, it addresses the role of sustainable investing and Environmental, Social, and Governance (ESG) criteria in guiding investment decisions in emerging markets, considering the significance of responsible investing practices.

By dissecting the opportunities, challenges, and factors influencing investment decisions in emerging markets, this chapter aims to provide insights into their potential for investors, the strategies for navigating risks, and the evolving dynamics that shape investment landscapes in these burgeoning economies.

CHAPTER 44: MENTAL HEALTH ON THE GLOBAL AGENDA: POLICIES AND CHALLENGES

Mental health has emerged as a critical issue on the global agenda, necessitating comprehensive policies and initiatives. This chapter explores the challenges and policy frameworks surrounding mental health on a global scale.

The chapter begins by analyzing the current landscape of mental health, addressing the prevalence of mental health disorders, the stigma associated with them, and the impact on individuals, societies, and economies.

Moreover, it scrutinizes the challenges in accessing mental health services, including disparities in access to care, inadequate resources, and the need for improved awareness and education.

The chapter navigates through the importance of policy interventions aimed at mental health promotion, prevention, and the provision of accessible and quality mental healthcare services.

Furthermore, it evaluates the global initiatives, such as the World Health Organization's Mental Health Action Plan, and international collaborations aimed at addressing mental health issues and fostering supportive environments.

Additionally, it addresses the significance of destigmatizing mental health, promoting mental well-being in workplaces, schools, and communities, and integrating mental health into broader healthcare systems.

By dissecting the challenges and policy approaches related to mental health on a global scale, this chapter aims to provide insights into the importance of prioritizing mental health, the barriers to effective mental healthcare, and the strategies necessary for fostering mental well-being worldwide.

CHAPTER 45: IMPACT OF AI ON EDUCATION AND LEARNING PARADIGMS

Artificial Intelligence (AI) is revolutionizing education, reshaping learning paradigms, and transforming the way knowledge is imparted and acquired. This chapter explores the profound impact of AI on education and its implications for learning methodologies.

The chapter begins by analyzing AI's role in personalized learning, adaptive learning platforms, and customized educational experiences tailored to individual student needs and learning styles.

Moreover, it scrutinizes the integration of AI-powered tools and algorithms in educational settings, such as intelligent tutoring systems, virtual assistants, and automated grading systems, enhancing teaching efficiency and learning outcomes.

The chapter navigates through the potential of AI in content creation, curriculum design, and the development of interactive and immersive learning experiences, fostering engagement and knowledge retention among students.

Furthermore, it evaluates the challenges and ethical considerations associated with AI in education, including concerns about data privacy, biases in AI algorithms, and the digital divide affecting access to AI-powered educational tools.

Additionally, it addresses the role of educators in adapting to AI-enabled teaching methods, the need for digital literacy skills among students, and the importance of balancing technological advancements with pedagogical approaches.

By dissecting the transformative impact of AI on education and learning paradigms, this chapter aims to provide insights into the opportunities for educational innovation, the challenges in implementing AI in educational systems, and the strategies for leveraging AI to enhance learning experiences and outcomes.

CHAPTER 46: DATA PRIVACY AND ETHICS IN THE DIGITAL AGE

Data privacy has become increasingly crucial in an era where digital interactions are pervasive. This chapter delves into the intricate realms of data privacy and ethics, examining their significance in the context of the modern digital landscape.

The chapter begins by exploring the evolution of data privacy, addressing the ethical considerations surrounding the collection, storage, and utilization of personal data by corporations, governments, and other entities.

Moreover, it scrutinizes the challenges posed by data breaches, cyberattacks, and the commodification of personal information, emphasizing the importance of robust data protection regulations and practices.

The chapter navigates through the ethical dilemmas in data usage, such as the balance between individual privacy rights and the need for data-driven innovation in fields like healthcare, artificial intelligence, and marketing.

Furthermore, it evaluates the role of regulatory frameworks, like the General Data Protection Regulation (GDPR), in safeguarding individuals' privacy rights and fostering responsible data governance.

Additionally, it addresses the importance of transparency, informed consent, and accountability in handling personal data, promoting ethical data practices and building trust among users.

By dissecting data privacy and ethics in the digital age, this chapter aims to provide insights into the complexities of protecting personal information, the ethical implications of data usage, and the imperative for responsible data management in a rapidly evolving digital landscape.

CHAPTER 47: RESILIENCE AND DISASTER MANAGEMENT IN URBAN CENTERS

Urban centers face increasing vulnerabilities to various disasters, necessitating robust resilience strategies and effective disaster management frameworks. This chapter delves into the critical aspects of building resilience and managing crises in urban environments.

The chapter begins by analyzing the unique challenges urban areas encounter regarding disaster preparedness, including the risks posed by natural disasters, infrastructure vulnerabilities, and the concentration of populations and assets.

Moreover, it scrutinizes the significance of urban resilience, emphasizing the need for proactive measures such as resilient infrastructure, emergency response plans, and community engagement to mitigate risks.

The chapter navigates through innovative approaches to disaster management in urban settings, including early warning systems, smart city technologies, and inclusive strategies that consider the needs of diverse urban populations.

Furthermore, it evaluates the role of governance structures, public-private partnerships, and international cooperation in enhancing urban resilience and effective disaster response.

Additionally, it addresses the importance of integrating climate adaptation measures, risk reduction strategies, and sustainable urban planning to build long-term resilience against diverse hazards.

By dissecting resilience and disaster management in urban centers, this chapter aims to provide insights into the challenges, strategies, and collaborative efforts necessary to build resilient cities capable of effectively responding to and recovering from disasters.

CHAPTER 48: PSYCHOLOGICAL IMPACTS OF SOCIAL MEDIA AND CONNECTIVITY

The pervasive use of social media and constant connectivity in the digital age has ushered in a new era of social interaction, yet it also brings forth significant psychological impacts. This chapter explores the complex and diverse psychological effects stemming from social media usage and constant connectivity.

The chapter begins by examining the positive aspects of social media, such as enabling connections, facilitating communication, and providing platforms for self-expression and community building.

Moreover, it scrutinizes the adverse psychological effects, including social comparison, anxiety, loneliness, and the detrimental impact on mental health caused by excessive use or negative interactions on social platforms.

The chapter navigates through the addictive nature of social media and its influence on self-esteem, body image, and the development of online personas, affecting individuals' perceptions of themselves and others.

Furthermore, it evaluates the implications of constant connectivity and the "always-on" culture, addressing the potential for burnout, reduced attention spans, and the blurring of boundaries between personal and professional lives.

Additionally, it addresses the importance of digital well-being, advocating for strategies to manage screen time, promote digital detox, and foster healthy online behaviors among individuals and communities.

By dissecting the psychological impacts of social media and connectivity, this chapter aims to provide insights into the complexities of digital interactions, the nuances of its effects on mental well-being, and the strategies necessary to navigate and mitigate the adverse psychological outcomes in the digital realm.

CHAPTER 49: BIOTECHNOLOGY REVOLUTION: ETHICS AND SCIENTIFIC PROGRESS

The rapid advancements in biotechnology have unlocked unprecedented possibilities for scientific progress, yet they also pose profound ethical considerations. This chapter delves into the intersection of ethics and scientific breakthroughs within the biotechnology revolution.

The chapter begins by exploring the transformative potential of biotechnology across various domains, including healthcare, agriculture, and environmental conservation, emphasizing the positive impact on human life and the environment.

Moreover, it scrutinizes the ethical dilemmas arising from gene editing technologies like CRISPR-Cas9, cloning, and genetic modification, discussing concerns related to ethics, morality, and the manipulation of life.

The chapter navigates through the ethical considerations in the use of biotechnology in enhancing human capabilities, addressing questions surrounding fairness, equity, and the potential societal divides it might create.

Furthermore, it evaluates the importance of regulatory frameworks, bioethics committees, and public engagement in guiding the ethical implications of biotechnological advancements.

Additionally, it addresses the ethical responsibilities of scientists, policymakers, and the public in shaping the trajectory of biotechnological innovation, advocating for a balance between scientific progress and ethical principles.

By dissecting the ethical dimensions of the biotechnology revolution, this chapter aims to provide insights into the ethical considerations inherent in scientific advancements, the necessity for responsible innovation, and the role of ethical frameworks in guiding the ethical development and application of biotechnology.

CHAPTER 50: FUTURE OF HEALTHCARE: TELEMEDICINE AND REMOTE CARE

The evolution of healthcare is witnessing a transformative shift towards telemedicine and remote care, redefining the delivery of medical services. This chapter explores the burgeoning role of telemedicine in shaping the future of healthcare.

The chapter begins by analyzing the advent of telemedicine and remote care technologies, highlighting their potential to provide accessible, cost-effective healthcare services regardless of geographical barriers.

Moreover, it scrutinizes the advantages of telemedicine, including increased patient convenience, reduced healthcare costs, and improved access to specialized medical expertise, especially in underserved areas.

The chapter navigates through the challenges and limitations of telemedicine, addressing issues of data security, regulatory frameworks, and the importance of establishing trust between patients and healthcare providers in a virtual environment.

Furthermore, it evaluates the integration of telemedicine into mainstream healthcare systems, discussing its role in complementing traditional in-person care, chronic disease management, and preventive medicine.

Additionally, it addresses the impact of telemedicine on healthcare disparities, underscoring the potential for equitable healthcare access through remote care technologies.

By dissecting the future trajectory of healthcare through telemedicine and remote care, this chapter aims to provide insights into the transformative potential of digital health solutions, the challenges in their widespread adoption, and the opportunities they present for revolutionizing healthcare delivery.

CHAPTER 51: CIRCULAR ECONOMY AND SUSTAINABLE CONSUMPTION

The concept of a circular economy has emerged as a beacon of hope in the realm of sustainable development. It offers a framework that aims to redefine our traditional linear economic model of 'take, make, dispose' into a regenerative system where resources are kept in use for as long as possible, with maximum value extracted during their use, and then responsibly recovered and regenerated at the end of their service life.

In the context of America's quest for sustainable practices, the adoption of a circular economy model stands as a pivotal strategy. This approach not only addresses the environmental challenges posed by resource depletion and waste accumulation but also offers economic benefits by fostering innovation, creating new job opportunities, and minimizing the reliance on finite resources.

To truly embrace a circular economy, a fundamental shift in consumption patterns is imperative. Sustainable consumption involves not just the utilization of eco-friendly products but also encompasses a holistic approach that encourages conscious purchasing decisions, reduced waste generation, and the promotion of reuse and recycling initiatives.

In the American landscape, initiatives promoting sustainable consumption are gaining traction. From eco-friendly product lines by major corporations to grassroots movements advocating for minimalism and waste reduction, there is a growing awareness of the need for responsible consumption habits. Policies supporting sustainable practices, such as extended producer responsibility and incentives for recycling, are also playing a crucial role in steering the country towards a more circular and sustainable economic model.

However, challenges persist in achieving widespread adoption of circular economy principles. These include overcoming infrastructural barriers, changing consumer behavior entrenched in a culture of disposability, and navigating complex supply chains. Collaborative efforts among governments, industries, consumers, and communities are vital to surmount these obstacles and drive the transition towards a circular economy successfully.

The journey towards a circular economy and sustainable consumption in America is a multifaceted endeavor requiring commitment, innovation, and collaboration across sectors. By fostering a culture of responsible consumption and embracing circularity, the nation can pave the way for a more resilient, resource-efficient, and environmentally conscious future.

CHAPTER 52: TRANSFORMATIVE POWER OF CULTURAL DIPLOMACY

Cultural diplomacy serves as a bridge connecting nations through the exchange of arts, ideas, language, and traditions. In the context of America's global engagement, cultural diplomacy wields a transformative power that transcends political boundaries and fosters mutual understanding, respect, and cooperation among diverse cultures.

The United States, with its rich tapestry of cultures stemming from its immigrant roots, has long recognized the potential of cultural diplomacy in shaping international relations. From educational exchange programs like Fulbright to cultural festivals, art exhibitions, and music tours, America has utilized various avenues to showcase its diversity and promote dialogue on a global stage.

Cultural diplomacy acts as a soft power tool, wielding influence through attraction rather than coercion. It helps in breaking down stereotypes, dispelling misconceptions, and building people-to-people connections that transcend diplomatic formalities. Through initiatives like the Peace Corps, cultural exchange programs, and hosting international events, the U.S. has been able to foster cross-cultural empathy and appreciation, laying the groundwork for stronger diplomatic ties.

The digital age has further amplified the reach and impact of cultural diplomacy. Social media platforms, online collaborations, and virtual cultural exchanges have facilitated instant connectivity, allowing for the dissemination of cultural expressions worldwide. The use of digital mediums has enabled broader participation and engagement, transcending geographical boundaries and facilitating dialogue among diverse populations.

However, the efficacy of cultural diplomacy also encounters challenges. Cultural differences, political tensions, and differing worldviews can sometimes hinder the smooth exchange of ideas and values. Moreover, balancing cultural promotion with respect for local traditions and customs remains a delicate task, requiring nuanced approaches and sensitivity to diverse perspectives.

Despite challenges, the transformative potential of cultural diplomacy remains undeniable. It has the ability to build trust, promote mutual respect, and lay the groundwork for meaningful collaborations in addressing global challenges. By embracing cultural diplomacy as a cornerstone of its foreign policy, America can continue to foster connections, bridge divides, and contribute to a more peaceful and interconnected world.

CHAPTER 53: EVOLVING ROLE OF NON-GOVERNMENTAL ORGANIZATIONS (NGOS)

Non-Governmental Organizations (NGOs) have evolved into pivotal players in addressing societal challenges, filling gaps in governance, and driving positive change across various spheres. In the American context, NGOs play a multifaceted role in shaping policies, advocating for social causes, delivering humanitarian aid, and promoting civic engagement.

One of the most notable shifts in the role of NGOs is their transition from being mere service providers to becoming active agents of change. NGOs now engage in policy formulation, collaborating with governments and international bodies to influence decisions and shape agendas. Their expertise, grassroots connections, and ability to mobilize communities make them valuable contributors to policy discussions, often advocating for marginalized voices and pressing social issues.

Moreover, NGOs serve as watchdogs, holding governments and

corporations accountable. Through research, monitoring, and advocacy, they shine a light on issues ranging from human rights abuses to environmental degradation, prompting action and demanding accountability from the authorities and institutions responsible.

In recent years, technology and social media have revolutionized the way NGOs operate. These tools have expanded outreach, facilitated fundraising, and enabled rapid response during crises. Online platforms serve as avenues for raising awareness, mobilizing support, and fostering global networks, empowering NGOs to connect with a broader audience and amplify their impact.

However, the evolving landscape presents challenges for NGOs. Increased scrutiny regarding transparency, accountability, and effectiveness has led to a call for greater organizational transparency and efficiency. Additionally, the proliferation of NGOs has created a crowded space, sometimes resulting in competition for funding and resources.

Despite these challenges, the role of NGOs continues to evolve, adapting to the changing needs of society. Collaborations between NGOs, governments, and the private sector are becoming more common, emphasizing the importance of collective action in addressing complex challenges such as climate change, poverty, and healthcare.

Looking ahead, the future of NGOs in America and globally hinges on their ability to innovate, collaborate, and adapt to a rapidly changing world. As catalysts for social change, NGOs stand poised to continue their crucial role in advocating for human rights, advancing sustainable development goals, and championing the voices of the marginalized and vulnerable populations.

CHAPTER 54: THE INFLUENCE OF BIG DATA IN MARKET DYNAMICS

The advent of the digital era has brought about a significant shift in the way businesses operate and compete. One of the most profound transformations lies in the utilization of big data, fundamentally altering market dynamics and strategies across industries.

Big data, characterized by vast amounts of information collected from various sources, offers unparalleled insights into consumer behavior, market trends, and operational patterns. This wealth of data, when analyzed and interpreted effectively, empowers businesses to make informed decisions, optimize processes, and tailor their offerings to meet evolving consumer demands.

In the American market landscape, big data has become a game-changer for companies seeking a competitive edge. From retail and finance to healthcare and entertainment, industries are leveraging big data analytics to gain a deeper understanding of their customers, predict market trends, and personalize their products and services.

The use of data analytics tools, machine learning, and artificial intelligence has revolutionized marketing strategies. Companies can now segment their audience more precisely, craft targeted advertising campaigns, and enhance customer experiences based on personalized preferences, thereby increasing engagement and fostering brand loyalty.

Moreover, big data has reshaped supply chain management. Advanced analytics enable businesses to optimize inventory levels, streamline logistics, and forecast demand more accurately, reducing costs and improving operational efficiency.

However, the widespread adoption of big data also raises concerns regarding privacy, security, and ethical considerations. The collection and utilization of vast amounts of personal information raise questions about data protection and the responsible use of consumer data, necessitating robust regulations and ethical frameworks to safeguard individuals' privacy rights.

The influence of big data in market dynamics is poised to continue growing. As technologies advance and data collection methods become more sophisticated, businesses will increasingly rely on data-driven insights to stay competitive and adapt to rapidly changing market conditions. Striking a balance between innovation, consumer privacy, and ethical use of data will be imperative in navigating the evolving landscape shaped by big data.

CHAPTER 55: ROLE OF WOMEN IN ECONOMIC EMPOWERMENT

The role of women in economic empowerment is not just a matter of equality; it's a critical driver of sustainable development and inclusive growth. In the American landscape and globally, empowering women economically has shown to have profound positive impacts on societies, economies, and the well-being of families.

Despite strides forward, gender disparities persist in various facets of the economy. Women, particularly in some regions and industries, face barriers to entry and advancement in the workforce. Factors such as unequal pay, limited access to education and healthcare, lack of representation in leadership roles, and cultural biases continue to impede women's full participation in the economy.

Efforts to address these challenges are underway. Initiatives promoting education and vocational training for women, access to financial resources, mentorship programs, and policies supporting work-life balance are instrumental in fostering economic empowerment. These efforts not only benefit individual women but also contribute significantly to the overall economy by unlocking untapped potential and driving innovation.

The role of women entrepreneurs is increasingly recognized as a catalyst for economic growth. Women-owned businesses contribute substantially to job creation and economic dynamism. Supporting female entrepreneurs through access to capital, networks, and business development opportunities is key to unlocking their entrepreneurial potential and fostering a more inclusive economy.

Moreover, diverse representation in leadership positions is crucial. When women are adequately represented in decision-making roles, diverse perspectives are brought to the table, leading to more innovative and inclusive policies and strategies.

In recent years, the digital revolution has provided new avenues for women's economic participation. Online platforms and remote work opportunities have enabled flexibility, allowing women to overcome some traditional barriers and participate in the economy on their terms.

Yet, there's more work to be done. Sustained efforts are needed to break down systemic barriers, challenge stereotypes, and create an environment where women have equal opportunities to thrive in all sectors of the economy. This requires collaboration between governments, businesses, civil society, and individuals to create an ecosystem that fosters gender equality and economic empowerment for women.

Ultimately, the economic empowerment of women isn't just a matter of fairness; it's an investment in a more prosperous and equitable society. When women are empowered economically, the benefits ripple through communities, economies, and future generations, creating a more vibrant and inclusive world for all.

CHAPTER 56:
GREEN FINANCE
AND SUSTAINABLE
INVESTMENT

The pursuit of sustainability has extended beyond mere environmental considerations; it has become a cornerstone of financial decision-making. Green finance and sustainable investment practices have emerged as powerful tools in reshaping the global economy towards a more environmentally conscious and socially responsible future.

In America and across the globe, there's a growing recognition that traditional investment models need to evolve to address pressing environmental challenges. Green finance encompasses a range of financial products, mechanisms, and investment strategies aimed at fostering sustainable development, reducing carbon footprints, and promoting eco-friendly initiatives.

Sustainable investing integrates environmental, social, and governance (ESG) criteria into investment decisions. It goes beyond seeking financial returns; it aims to generate positive social or environmental impacts while delivering competitive financial performance. ESG factors are considered in the assessment of the long-term sustainability and ethical impact of investments, driving capital towards companies committed to responsible business practices.

The concept of green bonds, for instance, has gained momentum. These bonds finance projects with environmental benefits, such as renewable energy, clean transportation, or sustainable infrastructure. Additionally, impact investing channels funds into businesses and projects that aim to address social or environmental issues while generating financial returns.

Financial institutions, including banks and investment firms, are increasingly integrating ESG principles into their policies and strategies. Investors are demanding transparency and accountability, prompting companies to disclose their sustainability practices and risks associated with climate change, social impact, and governance issues.

However, challenges persist in the realm of green finance. Standardization of ESG metrics, ensuring the authenticity of 'green' investments, and defining universal guidelines for sustainable practices remain areas that require further development. Regulatory frameworks and incentives are necessary to encourage more extensive adoption of sustainable investment practices across industries.

Yet, the momentum towards green finance and sustainable investment continues to grow. The commitment from governments, businesses, investors, and consumers towards building a more sustainable future is evident. By aligning financial decisions with sustainability goals, the trajectory of global markets can be steered towards a path that not only benefits investors but also promotes environmental stewardship and social well-being for generations to come.

CHAPTER 57: AI IN CLIMATE CHANGE SOLUTIONS AND ENVIRONMENTAL MONITORING

Artificial Intelligence (AI) has emerged as a potent ally in combating climate change and advancing environmental monitoring efforts. Its application across various domains, from predicting climate patterns to optimizing resource management, holds immense potential in addressing the challenges posed by environmental degradation.

In the realm of climate change, AI-driven predictive models play a pivotal role. These models analyze vast datasets, including historical climate data and real-time observations, to forecast changes in weather patterns, sea levels, and ecosystem behavior. Such predictive analytics empower policymakers, scientists, and environmentalists with valuable insights to devise proactive strategies for mitigating the impacts of climate change.

Furthermore, AI contributes to optimizing energy systems and resource management. Smart grids, enabled by AI algorithms, enhance the efficiency of energy distribution by predicting demand, optimizing supply routes, and integrating renewable energy sources effectively. This not only reduces carbon emissions but also promotes the utilization of sustainable energy alternatives.

AI-driven solutions also bolster environmental monitoring and conservation efforts. Drones equipped with AI-enabled sensors can survey and monitor biodiversity, track deforestation, and detect illegal activities such as poaching and logging in remote areas. These technologies aid conservationists in preserving fragile ecosystems and endangered species by providing real-time data and actionable insights.

Moreover, AI-powered precision agriculture revolutionizes farming practices. By analyzing data related to soil health, weather conditions, and crop patterns, AI algorithms assist farmers in making informed decisions about irrigation, fertilization, and pest control. This optimization not only increases agricultural productivity but also minimizes environmental impacts by reducing resource wastage.

However, the integration of AI in climate change solutions and environmental monitoring is not without challenges. Issues regarding data quality, bias in algorithms, and ethical considerations in AI applications need to be addressed. Additionally, accessibility and affordability of AI technologies pose barriers to their widespread adoption, especially in less developed regions.

Nonetheless, the synergies between AI and environmental conservation are promising. Continued research, investment, and collaboration among stakeholders are crucial to harness the full potential of AI in addressing climate change and safeguarding the planet's ecosystems. By leveraging AI technologies responsibly, humanity can strive towards a more sustainable and resilient future for our planet.

CHAPTER 58: GLOBAL CHALLENGES IN CYBERSECURITY GOVERNANCE

In an increasingly interconnected world, cybersecurity has emerged as a critical concern, transcending borders and posing complex challenges to governments, businesses, and individuals alike. The governance of cybersecurity faces multifaceted global challenges stemming from the rapid evolution of technology, the interconnectedness of digital systems, and the ever-evolving threat landscape.

One of the foremost challenges in cybersecurity governance is the dynamic nature of cyber threats. Cyberattacks constantly evolve in sophistication, utilizing advanced techniques such as ransomware, phishing, and zero-day exploits. These threats target critical infrastructure, financial institutions, healthcare systems, and even democratic processes, necessitating robust defenses and adaptive strategies.

Moreover, the borderless nature of cyberspace complicates governance efforts. Traditional governance structures often struggle to keep pace with the transnational nature of cyber threats. Coordination and collaboration among nations are essential, yet geopolitical tensions, varying regulatory frameworks, and differing priorities hinder global consensus on cybersecurity standards and regulations.

Another significant challenge revolves around the protection of data privacy and individual rights. As digital systems accumulate vast amounts of personal information, concerns about data breaches, surveillance, and misuse of data have escalated. Balancing security measures with the protection of privacy rights poses a constant dilemma in cybersecurity governance.

The shortage of skilled cybersecurity professionals further exacerbates the challenge. There's a global demand for qualified cybersecurity experts capable of understanding complex threats and implementing robust defense mechanisms. Addressing this shortage requires investments in education, training, and fostering a cybersecurity workforce equipped to tackle evolving threats.

Cybersecurity governance also faces challenges regarding the security of emerging technologies like artificial intelligence, Internet of Things (IoT), and quantum computing. These technologies bring unprecedented opportunities but also introduce new vulnerabilities that can be exploited by cyber adversaries, necessitating proactive security measures and regulations.

Effective cybersecurity governance demands a collaborative approach involving governments, private sector entities, academia, and international organizations. Establishing norms, standards, and protocols for cybersecurity, promoting information sharing, and investing in research and development are crucial steps toward bolstering global cyber defenses.

However, achieving consensus among diverse stakeholders and navigating the complexities of geopolitics and differing priorities remain significant hurdles. The need for international cooperation, information sharing mechanisms, and a collective commitment to strengthening cybersecurity defenses is paramount in addressing the global challenges in cybersecurity governance.

As cyber threats continue to evolve and grow in sophistication, addressing these challenges will require sustained efforts, innovative solutions, and a shared commitment to fortify the digital infrastructure and protect against malicious cyber activities on a global scale.

CHAPTER 59: INNOVATIVE APPROACHES TO ADDRESSING GLOBAL POVERTY

The fight against global poverty demands innovative and multifaceted approaches that go beyond traditional aid models. In recent years, there has been a growing recognition that tackling poverty requires not just financial aid but also sustainable, community-driven solutions that empower individuals and communities to lift themselves out of poverty.

Social entrepreneurship has emerged as a powerful force in addressing poverty. Innovative business models that combine profit-making with social impact aim to address pressing social issues while creating sustainable livelihoods. These enterprises focus on sectors such as healthcare, education, clean energy, and microfinance, offering solutions tailored to the needs of underserved communities.

Microfinance and microcredit initiatives have also played a transformative role in poverty alleviation. Providing small loans and financial services to individuals who lack access to traditional banking has empowered countless entrepreneurs, particularly women, to start businesses, generate income, and improve their families' standard of living.

Technology has proven instrumental in addressing poverty on a global scale. Mobile banking, for example, has expanded financial inclusion, allowing individuals in remote areas to access banking services and conduct transactions, thereby enhancing economic opportunities and resilience.

Moreover, education is widely recognized as a key factor in breaking the cycle of poverty. Innovative educational initiatives, such as online learning platforms, vocational training programs, and initiatives leveraging technology for remote education, are providing avenues for skill development and empowerment, particularly in underserved regions.

Social safety nets and targeted poverty reduction programs remain crucial. Governments and international organizations implement cash transfer programs, food security initiatives, and healthcare interventions to provide immediate relief and improve the well-being of the most vulnerable populations.

However, challenges persist. Inequalities, systemic barriers, and lack of access to basic resources continue to hinder poverty alleviation efforts. Addressing these challenges demands a holistic approach that combines innovative solutions with effective governance, investment in education and healthcare, and policies that foster inclusive economic growth.

Collaboration between governments, NGOs, private sector entities, and local communities is essential in advancing innovative approaches to address global poverty. By fostering an ecosystem that supports entrepreneurship, education, technology, and sustainable development, the world can strive towards more equitable societies where poverty becomes an exception rather than the norm.

CHAPTER 60: THE NEXT FRONTIER: ETHICS AND REGULATION IN SPACE EXPLORATION

As humanity's foray into space exploration accelerates, the necessity for ethical considerations and robust regulatory frameworks becomes increasingly vital. The vastness of space and the potential for significant discoveries bring forth unique challenges that necessitate thoughtful contemplation on ethical boundaries and governance.

One of the primary ethical considerations revolves around environmental impact. As missions venture beyond Earth, the preservation of celestial environments becomes crucial. Preserving the pristine nature of celestial bodies and preventing contamination, inadvertent interference, or disruption of indigenous ecosystems must be a priority in space exploration.

Another ethical frontier involves ensuring the responsible utilization of space resources. As technologies advance to extract minerals or establish human settlements on celestial bodies, questions arise regarding equitable access, sustainable resource extraction, and the prevention of exploitative practices that could lead to conflicts or inequality.

Furthermore, the potential discovery of extraterrestrial life raises ethical dilemmas. Protocols for handling and studying potential life forms or ecosystems on other planets must be established to prioritize scientific inquiry while adhering to ethical standards to avoid contamination or irreversible damage.

The absence of a universal regulatory framework for space activities poses challenges. While international agreements like the Outer Space Treaty exist, they lack comprehensive guidelines for emerging space endeavors. Issues such as space debris management, property rights, and jurisdictional matters in space require clearer regulations and international cooperation.

Commercial space ventures add another layer of complexity. Companies entering the space sector necessitate ethical guidelines regarding ownership of intellectual property, responsible advertising, and adherence to safety standards to avoid exploiting space for profit at the expense of ethical principles.

Ethical considerations in space exploration also encompass inclusivity and representation. Ensuring diversity in the workforce and representation in decision-making processes is crucial for fostering inclusivity and equity in the space industry, enabling a wide array of perspectives to contribute to ethical decision-making.

Addressing these ethical frontiers in space exploration demands collaboration among governments, space agencies, scientific communities, and ethicists. Establishing clear, universally accepted guidelines and regulations that balance scientific progress with ethical responsibility will be paramount in navigating the uncharted territories of space while upholding ethical values. As humanity ventures further into the cosmos, upholding ethical standards will be key in ensuring that space exploration remains a venture for the collective benefit of all.

Conclusion:

As we conclude our expedition through the chapters of "America's Global Odyssey: Pioneering New Horizons, Shaping Tomorrow," we find ourselves at the culmination of an illuminating journey. This odyssey has unveiled the intricate layers that constitute America's indelible imprint on the global canvas.

From historical precedence to contemporary challenges, our exploration has dissected the multifaceted dimensions that define America's role in shaping our interconnected world. Each chapter delved into critical themes: from geopolitical dynamics and economic intricacies to technological advancements and ethical frontiers, offering a comprehensive insight into America's global narrative.

Beyond analysis lies a deeper truth—an understanding that

America's narrative is interwoven with the destinies of nations worldwide. It is a narrative of resilience, adaptation, and innovation, converging with the shared aspirations of a global community.

As we navigate through the landscapes of cultural diplomacy, cybersecurity governance, sustainable investment, and ethical advancements in technology, we recognize that America's future is intricately linked to collaborative endeavors on a global scale.

"America's Global Odyssey" transcends national boundaries. It is an invitation to ponder, collaborate, and aspire toward a future that harnesses the collective potential of nations. Thought-provoking, engaging, and insightful, this odyssey illuminates the complexities of America's global presence and fosters a vision for a world that is collective, adaptive, and inclusive.

As we conclude this expedition, may the insights gleaned from these pages serve as a compass—a guiding light toward a tomorrow where collaborative efforts shape a resilient, innovative, and inclusive global landscape. This odyssey is not just a narrative of America—it is an endeavor to unravel the aspirations that resonate within nations, shaping the contours of a promising future for all.

9 7 9 8 8 8 7 0 3 3 3 7 8 6